Parent Code of Conduct

Theresa Roulhac Proctor

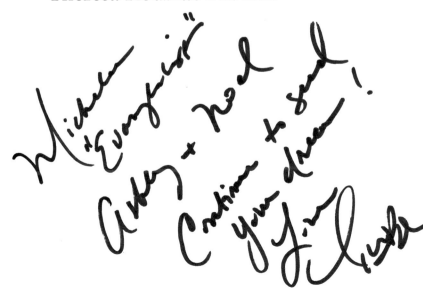

Theresa Michelle Enterprises, LLC
www.parentcodeofconduct.com
Cover art by Integrity Printing

Library of Congress Cataloging-in Publication Data:
Proctor, Theresa.
Parent Code of Conduct/Theresa Roulhac Proctor
p.cm

2014907771

ISBN: 978-0-692-20549-5

DEDICATION

God and
I also dedicate this book to my son…Omar
I love you dearly and thank God for your life which will continue to
positively impact the nation.
It is my prayer that you operate with the wisdom of God in all you do and
live a life pleasing to the Lord.
.

CONTENTS

ACKNOWLEDGMENTS

God, you are my everything! Without you, I am nothing. With you all things are possible and I will eternally serve you.

My husband, Benjamin, I thank you for your unwavering support and love. I love you so much! Mom and Dad, thank you for encouraging me to not be my best…but to be God's best. To my sisters and brothers, you are my inspiration and I love and appreciate you tremendously.

Bishop Abraham and Loretta Mitchum, your prayers, love and godly insight will forever remain in my heart. You have taught me the significance of reverence and righteousness. I honor and love you both immensely. The New Jerusalem family, thank you!

To my Pastors, Drs. Mike and Dee Dee Freeman, your lessons and wisdom have helped me to access fulfillment and success. Through your leadership, I continue to embrace a spirit of excellence in every area of my life. Pastor Dwayne Freeman and the Spirit of Faith family, thank you!

Dr. Traci Lynn and the Traci Lynn family, I thank God for the business opportunity that has transformed my life. Dr. Lynn, your mentorship has challenged me to become all that God predestined for my life.

To my Editor, Steve Avelleyra, thank you for your support of this work.

Celeste Wilson, thank you for all the long hours and creativity you have sown into this literary work. I thank God for your life.

Southern Management Corporation and the SMC family, the wealth of knowledge I gained with you was priceless. Thank you.

A big thank you to all of my friends and family who continue to love, pray and support me along the way. To all of you reading, I also acknowledge your support as you help spread this message "Parent Code of Conduct" throughout the nation. Together we will positively impact the lives of others.

Introduction

This book has taken me a little over three years to write. Have you ever felt there was something you needed to do, but you were a bit nervous of the impact or you may have allowed distractions to interrupt the plans of God? There has to come a time in your life when you become a part of "Generation Get it Done." Whatever you have been putting off, here is my advice: JUST DO IT! Don't allow perfection to paralyze you. It may not be the best time; a void of financial support might be occurring; or you don't think you are the one for the assignment. But let me say this to you: "It is the right time. You are the one, so make it happen!"

I was only at 25 weeks during my pregnancy when I gave birth to my son, Omar. He weighed 1lb 9oz., which equated to roughly 707 grams at the beginning of his three-month hospital stay. Those three months were extremely God-trusting moments. Those who wait upon the Lord shall renew their strength. My strength needed daily renewal. I recall receiving a phone call from the head nurse early in the morning. She said, "I know you will be here shortly and I want to share something with you…I don't want you to be alarmed when you walk in." I replied, "Ok, please share the details." The nurse told me they had a challenging time finding another area on Omar's body for an IV, so they had to place the IV in his scalp. I begin to feel like I was going to faint at the thought of a needle in my baby's head. However, I was thankful she gave me heads up, (literally heads up). Omar suffered from epilepsy and had seizures up until the age of ten. I was told by doctors the chance of his survival was low. I continued to trust God through the tears and trials. We--my husband and I--discovered after testing that Omar also had cerebral palsy and autism. Please get your child tested if you notice developmental delays or if your baby is having difficulty with processing information. For additional information

use the following sites as resources: www.autismspeaks.org or
www.autism-society.org. Early intervention has supported our family
tremendously. However, I was not moved by the reports of the
doctor. We continued to press towards victory. Although I am
aware of Omar's challenges, I have never given him a pass. A pass
to be mediocre or releasing him from his responsibilities is not in
my vocabulary. It is understood that he may not have the capability
to perform certain tasks or fully understand certain processes. I
have learned to adjust my delivery which we have highlighted in
the book.

After spending Christmas in the hospital with a tiny cute decorated
Christmas tree, Omar was discharged from the hospital in January
of 1997. He may have given up his bed at the hospital, but the
travels to the hospital and doctors were quite frequent. I thought
the hospital management would have at least offered me an
opportunity to join the staff as much as I was there. I remember the
nights Omar slept with a breathing machine; I could not go through
the night without getting up to check on him several times. We
moved his crib in our room and there would be times I would stare
at him to watch his chest move up and down.

As Omar began to reach his toddler years, we initially thought he
was being a typical active child. When he grew older, the activity
did not cease. One Saturday, his dad took him to the barber shop.
How cute: father and son getting their hair cut together, right?
Wrong! It was roughly 30 minutes when I noticed that they had
returned. I said, "Wow that was fast!" Yes, it was fast because
Omar was uncontrollable. He threw magazines, ripped and tore
pages completely out, and ran through the barber shop as if he was
outdoors. The gentlemen playing chess had to start over because
Omar dethroned all of the kings, queens and the remaining chess
pieces, knocking them to the shop floor.

During his preteen years, we were in search of a new school that would address Omar's behavioral challenges. This particular school, which shall remain nameless, required a three-day visit prior to the final decision of the enrollment process. On day two, I received a call from the administrator stating that Omar and another student had had a fight. This information was alarming because this was a new school visit. Wait, there is more! The administrator proceeded to tell me Omar stabbed the student in the back with a pencil. I asked, "Oh, my word! Please tell me the student is alright?" He responded, "Yes the student is fine. The pencil did not pierce through." The second thing I said to myself (after discovering the student was fine): "These parents are going to sue me, what am I going to do?" Thankfully, the parents accepted an apology. Inevitably, Omar did not receive the acceptance to the school. As you can clearly see, we experienced some serious challenges, and that's not even half of the story! As a result of the information I received, Omar is now an honor-roll student preparing for college.

Letter from Superintendent

Dear Parent:

The birth or adoption of your child was not an accident. Please understand that God has given you an incredible responsibility to serve as parent in their life. As you have discovered, this assignment at times may be challenging. However, don't lose heart (2 Corinthians 4:16–18) by focusing on the current conditions. Continue to saturate your life in the word of God and watch the manifestation of triumph in their life. As you read this book, many things will unfold and you will gain great clarity. Your questions will be answered and solutions will be revealed. Oftentimes, we need a stimulator to get us thinking differently, and reading this book will activate the wisdom of God in your thinking. When reading, be sure to use the journal (at the close of each chapter) to jot down your thoughts, trials and victories. There will be steps released specific to the needs of your child. These steps must be implemented with urgency. Please recognize, your obedience offers rewards.

"I have given you the power to get wealth." (Deuteronomy 8:18). This wealth does not solely apply to monetary gains, it applies to other areas of your life. When you stand on this scripture, you will experience wealth in your health, wealth in your peace, wealth in the life of your child and any areas lacking richness and abundance. There may have been times you've asked repeatedly why is your child demonstrating this type of behavior. My response to you…"You are chosen." God desires that you lean on him; he would like to receive the glory for the shift that is about to take place in the life of your child. You can handle this with God because all things are possible. God has allowed this to happen because you have everything inside of you to create a successful outcome. I recall a physically-challenged gentleman sharing with the proper mindset, you have the authority to shift a disability into an ability. Also be reminded that every good thing comes from your heavenly father.

Now, the first thing we will do is set a date to complete this reading. There must be a commitment to read this book entirely to get the fullness and harvest of implementing the codes. While the information discussed in this book will directly address your parenting, please don't be surprised when it helps to support your marriage, relationship with others or on-the-job situations. This book has an assignment: to heal, to restore, and to renew. There is a journal included to denote the progress your child will make at home and school.

CHAPTER 1

PARENTS RIGHTS AND RESPONSIBILITES

God has entrusted you with an enormous responsibility to care and guide the life of another spirit being, which will foster an amazing human experience. Whether the birth, or the securing of guardianship of your child was voluntary or involuntary, it does not matter. Are you feeling frustrated? Frustration is a natural emotion that you must take authority over. The only reason frustration appears is a result of the investment you have in your child's life. You would never become frustrated about something you have not invested in. Bishop Abraham Mitchum shared with me, you can allow a bird to fly over your head. But, you must not let the bird land on your head and build a nest. This speaks to the thoughts that come into our minds. The emotion of frustration may attempt to control you, instead you have the right to control it. Your mind is the navigation to your future. Yet, we may encounter many moments of frustration, we have been gifted with this life. As we modify our perception to acknowledge that this assignment is without any hesitation a blessing from God, the value of the assignment increases. You possess great value within, and that gift to forge a deeper connection with your child is a priority.

Parenthood is an honor, and the rewards are limitless. As Parents, we should not allow what we see to dictate what we believe for our child. I can vividly recall receiving calls from Omar's school every week with the report of inappropriate behavior. The Principal suspended him once again for inappropriate behavior and I was literally crying out for support. I asked the Principal time after time if there were any resources or programs that can help me to overcome this challenge. Unfortunately, she offered no support or resources. Suspension had a hindrance towards Omar's academic success. It is designed to punish the student, although Omar was quite delighted to miss a few days of school periodically. After I shared my concerns, the Principal stated she was not aware of any programs but her staff needed a break. I was utterly shocked by her response. I had to ask her to repeat it. Guess what? She did just that!

I wrote a letter to the Pupil Services Worker, Regional Superintendent and the Superintendent. After receipt of my letter, the Principal was demoted to a more suitable role to complement her skill set. I found out later that I was not the only parent upset with the conduct of that principal. However, I was one of a few parents that placed my concerns in writing. The Board of Education received a couple of verbal complaints referencing her leadership, and my letter is exactly what was needed to make the transition occur. There were additional concerns the school was facing, however, no one took the time to place ink to the paper. It's our right as parents to place our concerns in writing. Be sure to follow the chain of command to give the appropriate people an opportunity to respond to your requests.

I like to refer to this process as "ink for change." Each time you place your ink to paper-- just as your paper changes from blank to filled – you have the same goal as it relates to the matter. I look forward to hearing your personal testimony as consequence of the new information you are receiving. The Parent Code of Conduct was certainly the driving force in my life.

Once my letter reached many different channels, I received an apology, coupled with support and resources. The administrators begin to evaluate Omar and to perform testing. They quickly discovered that he needed an IEP, which is an Individualized Education Program. The IEP creates an opportunity for teachers, parents, school administrators, related services personnel and students (when appropriate) to work together to improve educational results for children with disabilities.

Code of Conduct: Schedule a meeting with the teacher and administrators to discuss viable options to address the behavior of your child. Be the initiator of the solution, and schedule a meeting with them before they request one with you. During the meeting, inquire about a behavior plan, resources and

programs. Expect a change.

You have the right to Change!

"Everyone thinks of changing the world, but no one thinks of changing himself."

– Leo Tolstoy

This quote is fitting in all circumstances in which we desire difference. Oftentimes in relationships, such as parent and child, husband and wife or workplace relationships, when someone is not conducting themselves according to our desires, we attempt to change them. This is a natural reaction. Listen closely to the word "attempt." It is an unsuccessful attempt. We do not possess the muscle to change anyone outside of ourselves. As we begin to take inventory and change the raw materials in our lives to parcels of goods we want to see in the lives of others will be delivered.

There are things about you that must change. Change invites consistency. A consistent parent will birth a consistent child. That consistency must be filled with good works. The person that continually evolves has a huge appetite for growth. If you have no idea of the changes essential to your growth and development, take a quick survey by asking a couple of credible people. Ask

4

them, if there was one thing you would change about me what would it be? Definitely inquire with God, as he has all the answers. Stop reading for a moment…ask God to reveal the areas in your life that require change and wait for a response. At times, we will ask for guidance and avoid listening for the answers. After those areas are exposed to you, be thankful because this is your opportunity to create a better version of you through self-discovery. I attended an amazing parenting workshop hosted by my dear friend, Carolyn Washington, Founder of Sisters 4 Sisters, Inc. Dr. Lonise Bias, the guest speaker said, "Parents, don't try to beat yourself out of your child." Wow, that statement hit me. Oftentimes, children emulate the actions of their parents. What we fear the most will manifest in our child's life. What is also surprising, the parent does not necessarily need to be present in their life. There are generational actions that may be transferred down ancestry. How do we combat this? Let's continue to read.

"Parents never stop parenting regardless of the circumstances that may arise."

The challenges with Omar appeared to me as insurmountable, complicated and complex. Did I say complicated? It was complicated. I initially did not consider the changing of my behavior. This was not certainly about me, I did not stab a co-worker in the back at the office. I did not turn tables and chairs over when something did not go according to my preferences. How could my behavior positively impact my son's behavior? It was magnetic when I began to embrace this process of changing for the better. I noticed as I changed he gradually began to do the same. It was marvelous to witness. Your why will honor your standards and sustain your momentum. Don't settle for less when you were made for more. We understand why change is needed and settling is not an option. Push forward. If you are looking for change on the job, in your marriage or anywhere, you change and change will be inevitable.

Code of Conduct: As we become better examples for our children, we build a stream for all generational blessings to flow. Remove anything hindering the flow of blessings in your life and home. You have the right to change.

There may be instruction shared in this book that you may be afraid to do… with the fear of what others may think or say. Dr. Mike Freeman said, "Divorce yourself from the opinion of others." Your family's life greatly depends upon your obedience. Please do not be concerned about what others may say regarding your situation. Make a declaration not to allow fear, lack of time or unbelief stop you from executing the codes in this book. As you move without hesitation, those things will be purged.

Generally, when we encounter trouble with our children we become angry with them. I know I did. I would be so upset and disappointed with Omar when the administrators from his school would call me about his hostile behavior. I would repeatedly say to myself, "I did not raise him like this!" This is a good time to lean not to your own understanding, but in all of your ways acknowledge God for direction. Proverbs 3:5-6 freed me tremendously on many days because I did not know what to do. A place of ignorance within ourselves can be transfigured to a position of great wisdom with God.

"What we achieve inwardly will change outer reality."

- Plutarch

It is quite obvious you are seeking change, otherwise you would not be reading this book. You obtain directions from God by the receiving Holy Spirit, establishing a relationship with God, by reading and understanding his word, and prayer/thanksgiving to God. We do not have a right to be angry with our children. Anger will offer a state of instability and a lack of creativity. I had to start a physical and mental exercise each time I felt my temperature rising. My personal exercise consisted of inhaling, exhaling a few times, and then pulling out my bible to read a few comforting scriptures. This exercise took less than five minutes. When I had to leave my job to take a trip to the school for Omar, I arrived at the school calm, cool, collected, and concerned.

Code of Conduct: Develop a brief--five minutes or less--exercise to control undesirable emotions and stress.

I recall vividly one morning during prayer, I paused, and remained silent to listen to God. God shared with me to extend more love to my son. I was initially puzzled because I provide shelter, food, clothing, and limitless support to this child, what could more love look like? In my scripture reading, Jonah spoke about being rich in love. I understood right at that moment I was displaying an adequacy of love that could use an increase to richness. I received instructions to start sharing with Omar verbally words of love such as, "You are intelligent, thank you for listening to sound instructions" (Because I just didn't want him listening to any instructions – sound instructions only). "You are a man of God, I love you so much and you will fulfill your assignment from God." I said to Omar whatever the Holy Spirit gave me and of course with a loving smile. The key to this exercise is your heart, you MUST believe it in your heart and confess with your mouth. Continue to say it until it becomes real to you in your heart and it will become a reality. This is surely a perspective shifter. By demonstrating love in this way, we allow the invisible (no behavioral challenges) to impact the visible (the current behavioral challenges). I also began to hug him every morning and say, "Good morning, man of God." I could truly see he was feeling the richness of my love. Life was not designed for you to accept just anything. Love positions you to give and receive only the best. Here are words that will undoubtedly minister to you:

1 Corinthians 13:4-7

So no matter what I say, what I believe and what I do, I'm bankrupt without love.

Love never gives up

Love cares more for others than for self

Love doesn't want what it doesn't have

Love doesn't strut

Doesn't have a swelled head

Doesn't force itself on others

Isn't always "me first"

Doesn't fly off the handle

Doesn't keep score of the sins of others

Doesn't revel when others grovel

Takes pleasure in the flowering of truth,

Puts up with anything.

Trust God always,

Always look for the best,

Never looks back,

But keeps going to the end.

Every day before and after school, Omar and I would have exclusive time to discuss his day at school and anything else that may come up. The Holy Spirit shared with me to tell Omar whenever he felt like doing something inappropriate to ask God to help him be a good boy. The scripture I had Omar to recite daily Philippians 4:13 I can do all things through Christ which strengthens me. While in elementary, he received point charts to track his behavior daily. As I was picking him up from daycare, his little friend Courtney said to me Omar was on red today (red was bad behavior, yellow meant some distractions and green was great). Omar interrupted to tell me it was not true, he was on green today. During our ride home, he was eager to show off his point sheet. "Look Mom look! I told you I was on green today! Now, may I have a treat", Omar enthusiastically stated. I noticed the sheet did not have a date on it, only his name. I did not think much of it. When we arrived home and settled in, I began to look through Omar's backpack. I noticed another point chart dated for that date with red markings just as Courtney announced. After a few probing questions and the evidence of green marker ink on Omar's fingers, he bowed his head and confessed he did it. This 7 year old at the time tried me. Since my memory serves me correct, I did the same thing to my mom in high school. It's proven as you read earlier, our actions impact our children.

A few days later, Omar brought home a point chart with green. He promised me his teacher Mrs. Henderson completed it. He also revealed, there were times he thought about doing something bad. However he asked God to help him and recited his scripture, I can do all things through Christ which strengthens me.

Code of Conduct: Extend unconditional actions of love. Share verbally and physically with your child how much you love them. Spend time with them doing something they enjoy. Leave short notes around the house for them expressing your love and speaking life over them. Also give them instructions to combat any issues they are experiencing.

Journal

CHAPTER 2

DRESS

You may think this chapter is about the physical dress, it is not. It is totally surrounding your spiritual and mental dress. Unknowingly, we share some of the same parenting tactics our parents shared with us: good, bad or indifferent. In order to better our children, we must better ourselves. We have a lot on our plate and we have the authority to manage it with the help of the Lord. By the way, there are a few things on your plate that must be removed immediately. Take a look at your plate and assess what is weighing you down unnecessarily. Conduct a value assessment by asking yourself if this task is adding value to your life. If not, bless and release. I told you this book will help in multiple areas of your life. The reason I'm requesting a value assessment is because you may be thinking there are not enough hours in the day. Do you think for a moment that a loving God would not give you the essential hours to accomplish your daily tasks? He absolutely gave us the appropriate amount of hours, we just need to manage our priorities more efficiently.

Ephesians 6:11 Put on the whole armor of God, that ye may be able to stand against the wiles of the devil. In the book of Ephesians 6, it speaks about various pieces of apparel that one is required to wear daily as we live our lives. This armor includes truth, righteousness, peace, faith and salvation, which means living in right standing with God. Have you accepted God into your life? If not, now is a good time. Repeat this, "I believe in my heart and confess with my mouth that God raised Jesus from the dead. I am now saved!" Read Romans 10:9–10. Congratulations, and welcome to the family of God! Now, build your relationship with God by finding a good bible teaching church.

We should be equipped with the armor of God, because we have too much thrown on our plates to handle on our own. Have you said lately, "If I just had someone to help me I could get more done." This is the truth. You need God, I needed God and, I still need him. I remember while at work, my co-worker whispering, "Theresa, your son's school is calling again on line 4000." I said to myself, "Ok I can handle it." I picked up the phone and the voice on the other end was the school Administrator. She requested that I pick Omar up. He was suspended for hitting a teacher on her rear end. Tears began to roll down my cheek in pure discouragement as my head felt like it was about to hit my desk. I wiped the tears from my eyes and shared with the Administrator, "I will be there shortly." I got myself together and went to my car. I had to take a few minutes to exercise, I inhaled and exhaled and recited scriptures. Immediately a peace came over me because initially I was feeling so overwhelmed. Wait a minute! I have God on my side and I remembered one of my spiritual fathers Bishop Abraham Mitchum sharing with me "one with God is the majority." After reading the scriptures I said, "God I present my son to you. I thank you for your direction and guidance." Three scriptures that really helped me during this time of my life were:

Psalm 32:8 I will instruct thee and teach thee in the way which thou shalt go: I will guide thee with mine eye.

Proverbs 3:5-6 Trust in the Lord with all thine heart and lean not unto thine own understanding. In all thy ways acknowledge him and he shall direct our paths.

Psalm 23:1 The Lord is my shepherd and I shall not lack.

Repeat these scriptures and allow them to get into your heart and to believe them.

Code of Conduct: Write the scriptures down somewhere easily accessible that speak directly to your situation. Repeat the scriptures a minimum of three times daily (morning, afternoon and evening). Ask yourself how these scriptures speak to your situation to ensure there is a connection. This is how you stay dressed.

Journal

CHAPTER 3

ATTENDANCE

It is quite the normal nowadays to operate with a full plate. There is so much competing for our attention. Statistics state on average there are roughly 3,500 messages battling for our attention daily. I believe what you give attendance to gets your attention. As it relates to our children, they desire more of our attendance. We have to show up in their lives with laser focus. The Holy Spirit shared with me I was not present in my son's life. I had no idea what this meant. We were together all the time. I spent more time with him than anyone at least that is what I thought. I started to meditate on Omar's emotional needs. I thought to myself he knows I love him. But, the question was: Was I demonstrating my love on a deeper level?

Listen to the whispers or they will become screams

We must evaluate what is currently on our plate. "There are some things that must be removed." I had to repeat this sentence again because we become so consumed with the cares of life that we neglect what is really important. Pray and it will be revealed to you. It could possibly be a committee you are serving on, the triple threat (telephone, television and/or technology), take time to assess your plate and remove the unnecessary. Now that you have completed that process, you will take notice of greater things you are now available to accomplish. By establishing a greater consciousness, every morning before my son left for school, we did a few things:

1. Held hands to pray (I strongly believe in the power of prayer. Frequently, we would also ask Bishop Abraham Mitchum to pray for Omar. Bishop would lay hands and pray with Omar on countless Sundays during service. This has continued still today, my spiritual father Dr. Mike Freeman has prayed and laid hands on Omar as well.) Each morning I would speak greatness over Omar's life, thanked God for his protection and declared this day (and the rest of his life) will be good in Jesus name

2. Make declarations over their life verbally (he needed to hear these). "You will have a great day." "You will follow sound directions." "You will do well academically." "You're a man of integrity"

3. We created a simple affirmation to repeat easily. Omar's affirmation is "I can do all things through Christ that strengthens me." Philippians 4:13

4. Reiterate to them the power they possess. When

they cannot control their behavior, ask God for help. Matt 7:7 "Ask and you shall receive."

5. Workout. We did a short 10-minute exercise that consisted of running in place, jumping jacks and other simple maneuvers. I did this to help Omar burn some energy.

Also, make sure when preparing their breakfast that you do not use the microwave. If you are preparing cereal, be sure the amount of sugar is less than 10 grams. I recall speaking with my spiritual mom First Lady Loretta Mitchum, as she shared with me the importance of a healthy diet. She recommended that I remove the foods high in sugar, reduce the use of the microwave, and prepare fresh vegetables (eliminate the cans). When I began to incorporate this process, I noticed more great improvements. Please be reminded this is a process. Do not expect an overnight change. However, you should expect a change. Your child will perform at your level of expectation. We project onto our child that which we hope for ourselves as well. Be conscious of this. If you expect to receive a bad report, you will. If you expect they will only behave the first couple of hours in the day, they will. Expect only those things which are good. Whatever you focus on swells. Be sure your focus is positively driven. Micah 7:7 in The Message bible reads, "But me, I'm not giving up. I'm sticking around to see what God will do. I'm waiting for God to make things right. I'm counting on God to listen to me." Don't just hang in there, stick in there to know things will shift for the better soon. It's a process.

Code of Conduct: Establish a morning regiment that demonstrates your extension of undivided attention in their life. Practice this daily and they will adapt and positively respond to that special time with you. Find a credible youth mentoring group for your child to participate in. Positive external coaching reinforces all that you are sharing at home.

Attendance impacts your grade on the parent's report card. Our students have a percentage of the grade specifically set aside for attendance. By not showing up, the grade is unfavorably impacted. Our children need us to show up. I remember showing up at Omar's school only when the teacher called. I shifted my actions and begin to show up without a call. The first day I showed up, his eyes widened with surprise as I walked in the room. It looked as if he was taking an internal behavior assessment, "Did I hit anyone? No. Was I disruptive? No. Why is she here?" When he received a break, he walked up to me and said, "Mom, why are you here? I did not do anything." I replied with a hug, and said, "I'm here to congratulate you on your good behavior." IMPACTFUL!

By showing up without a call, I dismantled his thoughts of attention given only for derogatory behavior. You may also be thinking, "Theresa, my job is demanding and I cannot take the time off." You have what you say, if you continue to say you don't have the time you will never. Begin to speak with authority over your situation (sidebar – this may also be applied to promotion and income increase on the job or in your business). Show up to work earlier and ask if you can come in on the weekend for a couple of hours to supplement the hours needed to visit your child's school. You may need to apply discernment; the reason for your departure may need to remain confidential. Some supervisors may not be as understanding as others as a result of their childhood. Please use your discernment.

I also "showed up" at home. To be under the same roof with our children is not "showing up." To "show up" means to demonstrate unwavering attention. If you work from home, be mindful of how you show up. Set aside "show-up" time. This is the time where nothing else matters. Turn off everything (phone, television, etc.) and it's all about them. It is critical that we are mindful of the words we use as well. Example: you're on a call and your child attempts to ask a question. Oftentimes, the typical response is "Just one moment, I'm on an important call." Regardless of the delivery, we are sharing with our child the call is more important. When I became aware of my language, I began to speak differently. "You are so important to me and I can't wait to spend time with you." Thereafter, I began to set aside quality time with Omar, and this truly enhanced our relationship.

We cannot leave what is important to us, up to something or someone else. The "TVT" (Television, Video Games and Telephone) was not called to parent our children. The TVT is a team of potential distractions if abused. In thousands of cases, the TVT has taken the role of raising our children. Parenthood is a gift and assignment from God, however when we allow our children to become guided by "television hood," "video hood," or "telephone hood," it will begin to negate our parental responsibilities and will program their minds with undesirable waste. Dr. David Perlmutter, Board Certified Neurologist wrote in the Huffington Post: "By the time the typical American child finishes elementary school, he will have witnessed 8,000 murders on television, while 79 percent of Americans feel that TV violence helps precipitate real-life violent behavior. The average American child witnesses 20,000 30-second television commercials each year." Dr. Perlmutter also denoted 5 main areas of concern with reference to television and children:

1. Time spent watching TV displaces other types of creative and imaginative activities.

2. Television watching discourages reading.

3. Television watching discourages exercise.

4. Television advertising increases demand for material possessions.

5. Exposure to violence on television can increase aggressive behavior in some children.

I believe all five main areas of concern are accurate and may be the contributing factors of aggressive behavior. This may also be applied to video games and telephone engagement. Proverbs 4:23-26 (MSG) denotes: "Keep vigilant watch over your heart; that's where life starts." Don't talk out of both sides of your mouth; avoid careless banter, white lies, and gossip. Keep your eyes straight ahead; ignore all sideshow distractions. Watch your step, and the road will stretch out smooth before you. As you are in search of strategies to improve the behavior of your child, remove the distractions as the scripture suggests, it is relentlessly influential. Attendance is the appeal to desirable results.

"Love begins at home, and it is not how much we do… but how much love we put in that action."

– Mother Teresa

The weapon of your actions will model another

dimension of love in their lives. Love never fails. This time in your child's life they need your love more than ever. We must take an assertive approach in the stadium of love. Love will give you a winning advantage over what was attempting to strike you out of life. You will hit it out of the ballpark continually with love. Love will build whatever you need.

1 John 3:18 (KJV) "My dear children, let us not love in word, neither in tongue; but in deed and in truth."

While words offer encouragement and support, fruitful actions are demonstrative of love. In the morning, we are moving with the speed of light to get out of the house to work. Begin to take 3–5 minutes to sit and share with your child. Share how much they mean to you. Tell them how proud you are to be their parent and the fact that they are special. This action will dismiss the need for attention warranted by negative behavior. Some children will be disobedient to gain attention from others. However, when you provide that attention without the prompt of a negative occurrence it breaks the cycle…"BREAK the cycle!"

Show up to school, "just because." You will realize we do not have control to change anyone (not even our spouse). We have the influence to change ourselves. Changing you changes your environment, and once the environment is converted, people will desire to change themselves.

Let's discuss relationships for a moment. I attended Oprah's Life Class in Dallas, Texas. TD Jakes was the guest speaker. He said something that absolutely pierced my thinking. TD Jakes shared, if you love your child like you love your man, there would be less issues. This may also be applied to loving a woman greater than you love your child. It is understood that in marriage the husband and wife is always the priority. However, this excludes giving the parent a pass to dismiss attendance. Be mindful of the way you attend to all of your relationships.

Each relationship nurtures a strength or

weakness within you – Mike Murdock

Code: Remove the distractions, reduce the amount of hours significantly that your child spends with the TVT team. As a parent and guiding force, be certain to show up more in their lives. Encourage discussions about the shows they view as it relates to your family values. Encourage your child to become involved in reading programs, sports or hobbies. Schedule and commit to "Show up" time daily. Show love with your actions and expect a delightful change. Attendance is the key.

Journal

CHAPTER 4

PUNCTUALITY

Ecclesiastes 3:1 (KJV) "To every thing there is a season, and a time to every purpose under the heaven. Do you believe the harvest is greater in its proper season?" Of course it's the law of farming. We must be certain to understand the timeliness of the decisions we make. There may be a time when we want to react hastily. In some incidents the results of a quick response may or may not be fruit yielding.

Everything rises and falls on time. Punctuality builds and exposes discipline. Discipline or the lack thereof is witnessed by our children and passed down to generations. Punctuality is connected to behaviors. "Small disciplines repeated with consistency every day lead to great achievements gained slowly over time." – John Maxwell. If you reflect upon various areas in your life, consider the areas that could use greater discipline. Increase the discipline in the vital areas which will embark on additional matters of your life. I believe discipline demonstrated is a more powerful teaching than actual directives. It's been proven more is caught than taught. We must understand discipline, it is not emotionally driven. When you are committed to maximizing every moment, you are not going to perform based upon your feelings. There will be no excuses. As a matter of fact, you will allow it to be your reason and not your excuse to get it done. You will perform based upon your commitment and it starts with making a decision. We must count up the cost. Where you are today is the consequence of the decisions you made yesterday. Your destiny is only obedient to good decisions.

In summation, discipline is taking responsibility.

"The price of greatness is responsibility." – Winston Churchill. Would you like your child to be more responsible? Would you like the greatness within your child to rise to the surface for the world to recognize) (especially – at this moment with their teachers)? Desired results will be achieved when responsibility is established at home. The more responsibility and discipline we exhibit as parents, the best harvest is what we can expect from our seed. Time rules everything. William Shakespeare said "Better three hours too soon, than one minute too late."

The timing of our words and actions play a critical role in the development of our children. It is obvious our child embraces attention; in a timely manner let's make an effort to give our children the desires of their hearts. Uncover opportunities to celebrate good behavior immediately. This alone will diminish the plot of unwanted behaviors to gain attention. You may ask, "Theresa, how do I recognize my child?" Remember, you know your child better than anyone; just observe what makes them light up. There are intrinsic rewards and extrinsic rewards. Intrinsic rewards (within) are never motivated by gifts. They are rewarded by praise and a sense of progress and meaningfulness. Extrinsic rewards (outside) offer engagement through trips to their favorite restaurants, ice cream dates, amusement park visits, etc.

The reverse of punctuality is procrastination. Procrastination is planted with seeds of laziness and excuses that will grow leaves of frustration. Applying the wisdom of God will cause you to move with a sense of urgency. Remember I said your thinking will be stimulated to perform different actions with your child. You cannot afford to procrastinate. Punctuality releases frustration.

Psalm 90:12 denotes So teach us to number our days, that we may apply our hearts unto wisdom. When you discontinue procrastinating, you meet your purpose with punctuality. You are here on earth to fulfill your purpose as a parent and more. Be compelled to move now.

Code of Conduct: Enhance your priority management, discipline and responsibility. Drive behavior with recognition. Make a recognition list and practice it.

Journal

CHAPTER 5

DISRUPTIVE BEHAVIOR

It was Sunday afternoon, Bishop Abraham Mitchum just concluded an anointed Sunday message. I noticed Missionary James walking towards me. She asked how the family was. I released a deep sigh. I replayed the most recent telephone calls I received from Omar's school. The Principal notified me of the third suspension Omar was given as a result of his disruptive behavior, which included throwing chairs in the classroom, hitting other students, not following instructions and more. Let's not forget Omar slapping his lady teacher on the rear end with his hand. I responded to Missionary James with sadness, "I don't know what to do about Omar. He is out of control and I don't know what else to do. I have never desired to start him on medication because he would miss his childhood and be subjected to a zombie state of living. This is something I was not willing to do." Missionary James responded, "Well, Sister Theresa, as you lay aside the weight and the sin, God will honor your request." I was taken aback because what do my actions have to do with my son. We are two different individuals. How is it that what I do impacts the life of my child?

I began to meditate on that scripture, Hebrews 12:1 "Wherefore seeing we also are compassed about with so great a cloud of witnesses, let us lay aside every weight, and the sin which doth so easily beset us, and let us run with patience the race that is set before us." Sin never stops God, it barricades us from receiving. I now began to understand, although my son did not personally see or witness the sins I committed. The meaning of "witness" is a person or thing that affords evidence. Some evidence may be invisible and prominent simultaneously. In the aforementioned scripture, the weight comes before the sin, because the weight is meant to grip you down for the sin to occur. This was such an insightful message to me because I had literally no idea of the impact my actions had in the life of my son as it related to sin. I thank Missionary James for her boldness and compassion for my family, and I removed the barriers that continued to hinder or delay my answered prayers. Thank God for his grace. Please understand doing the right thing qualifies you for increase and answered prayers.

Your child is living off the decisions you make

I stood on Matthew 7:7, "Ask, and it shall be given you; seek, and ye shall find; knock, and it shall be opened unto you." Through this message I was now able to work from my truth to become more obedient to the word of God for the sake of my child.

Matthew 6:33 states, "But seek ye first the kingdom of God, and his righteousness; and all these things shall be added unto you." If you are looking for things to be added to your life, you just need to seek God and his righteousness. When you are in right standing with God, No's are not invited. There is nothing he will withhold from you. We should seek God through prayer and fasting. Your purpose and next steps are discovered in prayer. Setting aside daily prayer will fortify your faith and psychological armor. The amount of calls from Omar's school could have possibly diminished my faith. But God, prayer and fasting is sustaining. You enter into a new dimension of belief with prayer and fasting. Pastor Dwayne Freeman said, "Unbelief will stop the power from flowing." Doubt creates uncertainty. Your belief system plays a vital role in the manifestation of your prayers. Fasting is scheduled abstinence from eating or anything else that you find pleasurable. Fasting demonstrates to God that he is the priority in our lives. This was certainly not an option for me. It was and still remains as a requirement and lifestyle in my Christian journey.

There is something I have identified as "generational influence." This generational influence is quite evident in the interaction with our parents. There is a link between your relationship with your parents and the parental connection with your child. My awareness was enlightened when Omar, my mom and I were on vacation. When I noticed how I treated my parent directly triggered the way my child treated me, it was astonishing. I affectionately call my mother Madea, after the Tyler Perry's role. I strongly believe he sought my mom for the character references in the role of Madea. After an exciting day of fun, we were enjoying dinner and my mom began to ask me questions as if I was the head chef. I initially replied by stating, "That's a great question, I'm not sure." My lack of information did not withhold the questions from coming. Thereafter, I became a bit short in my responses and not as pleasant as I should have been. I did not refuel my tolerance tank on that day, the fuel light was on. Remember, evidence may be invisible or visible. In this case it was visible. Omar began to respond to me in the same manner as I responded to my mother. There may be an impediment of honor from your child due to a lack of honor to your parents. Ephesians 6:2-3 (MSG) shares with us, "Children, do what your parents tell you." This is only right.

"Honor your father and mother" is the first commandment that has a promise attached to it, namely, "so you will live well and have a long life." When you sow honor, you will reap virtue. There may be some areas in your life even outside of your child's disorderly behavior that presents a blockage. The honoring of your parents will release the flow. If I am speaking to you, place this book down right now and repent for your dishonor and pick up the phone and call your parents. Offer an immediate apology to your parents and vow to them from this day forth you will always honor them. If your parents have passed, repent and write an apology letter to them. You need this release, posture yourself to receive it.

Honor is recognized when the person feels esteemed according to their fondness.

Code of Conduct: Combat disruptive behavior by laying aside any sin in your own life. Constantly pray and fast. Honor your mother, father and others. All of the aforementioned will ultimately set you up to receive the desires of your heart.

Journal

CHAPTER 6

TRUANCY

"The action of staying away without good reason" defines the word "truancy." When we mediate on the definition of truancy, it makes us ponder on the various compartments of our life. It is imperative that we dismember and explore each area of our lives to uncover any areas in need of reconstruction. As shared in the last chapter, we discussed laying aside the sin to produce fruitful results. This cannot be said enough, our actions will eternally impact the lives of our children. As a side note, have you ever witnessed a child that has never spent a day in life with his/her father or mother? However, they emulate some of their parent's characteristics. It's amazing to me.

There is an area in your life in which you are truant and some areas show chronic truancy. This is an area you have neglected and avoided for whatever reason. I know you're in deep thought. Together let us scrutinize the various compartments of your life. Answer the following questions:

How often do I pray? (Do I ask God to bless my will or do I inquire about his will for my life?)

What is the frequency of my fasting aside of my ministry (church)?

How frequently do I refuel myself with inspiring information? (by reading/hearing)

When do I devote time to mediation? (time to think on things pure and pleasant)

How much time do I spend building a relationship with my children?

Does my life exhibit order?

Am I a good steward over my finances?

How do I treat my wife/husband? (This area should not be confused with the parenting department. Parenting and being a wife/husband serves as two separate areas)

This is an awesome way to start evaluating the truant areas of your life. When you are no longer absent in the areas discussed (or maybe some areas we did not discuss), you have the authority to place a demand on the seeds sown.

Here are steps to address the truancy:

1) Identify the area(s) in which you are absent.

2) Seek wise counsel from someone that you respect. This person of accountability will serve as your "Attendance Partner."

3) Schedule a conference (telephone or in person) with your "Attendance Partner" to share your findings.

4) Create a remedy or TEP (Truancy Elimination Plan) highlighting the steps to reduce and consequently eliminate the absenteeism.

5) Implement with urgency. (The quicker you move the sooner you can expect good results.)

Code: Identify the areas in your life that require your attention. Connect with an "Attendance Partner" to hold you accountable. Follow the above steps and expect victory.

Journal

CHAPTER 7

WEAPONS PERMITTED

"For the weapons of our warfare are not carnal, but mighty through God to the pulling down of strong holds." – 2 Corinthians 10:4

In this chapter, I will share four weapons permitted in the school of parenting.

I can recall several times questioning if my child was switched at birth. Surely, this was not my child acting so unruly. I mean he was just WILD! There was another occasion where Omar was fighting a student in class. The fight was so major, the school requested that I pick him up immediately. This day I could not leave work, so thankfully my friend Kinicia picked Omar up for me. I was fed up! In route to pick up Omar, I had a talk with myself with tears in my eyes. Yes, again. I cried many days. I said, "I'm not tolerating this any longer!" Do you talk back to yourself? I do. I replied back, "That's right, this is it!" When you become angry at your circumstance, this is when change takes place. What you tolerate, you cannot change. Anger is not a good emotion for anyone to carry, at that moment in my life it was real to me.

The weapons you need, you already possess. There are four weapons I had tucked away in my arsenal which I began to use. The weapons are mediation, word, heart and prayer with fasting. When I began to implement these strategies, I began to see another segment of change in my Omar's life.

The Weapon of Meditation

You must mediate on the change you desire to see in your child. See your child in the most positive light imaginable. Your imagination will escort you to the life that does not exist yet. Meditate on your child following sound directions, conducting themselves appropriately, and at the next parent/teacher conference, the administration looking at you with bright eyes of amazement. They have never witnessed a child's behavior changing to this degree without medication. Can you see it? Raise your thinking, I need you to see this in your mind first. Meditation ignites your mindsight. 3 John 1:2 "Beloved, I pray that you may prosper in all things and be in health, just as your soul prospers." Our children will oftentimes perform at our level of expectations. If we expect them to act disorderly, our wish has a good chance of becoming true. Think on the positive and expect the absolute best. This starts with expanding our thinking to a good place.

Whatever we expect with confidence becomes our own self fulfilling prophesy – Dr. Traci Lynn

Code of Conduct: Take 5 minutes each morning to meditate on this vision, confess with your mouth and believe it in your heart. It's done.

The Weapon of Word

God gave us his word as a guide to navigate through the good and the not so pleasant. We must study, rightly divide and confess the word of God. You cannot confess and stand on that which you don't know. Take a moment to go through the bible and extract scriptures that apply to your needs. Below are some good ones to start with…

Isaiah 54:17 "No weapon that is formed against thee shall prosper; and every tongue that shall rise against thee in judgment thou shalt condemn."

Philippians 4:13 I can do all things through Christ which strengtheth me.

2 Timothy 3:16-17 – "All scripture is given by inspiration of God, and is profitable for doctrine, for reproof, for correction, for instruction in righteousness": 17 "That the man of God may be perfect, thoroughly

furnished unto all good works."

Ephesians 6:4 "And, ye fathers, provoke not your children to wrath: but bring them up in the nurture and admonition of the Lord."

Matthew 3:17 "And lo a voice from heaven, saying, this is my beloved Son, in whom I am well pleased."

1 Peter 4:8 "And above all things have fervent charity among yourselves: for charity shall cover the multitude of sins."

Exodus 20:12 "Honour thy father and thy mother: that thy days may be long upon the land which the LORD thy God giveth thee."

Colossians 3:20 "Children, obey your parents in all things: for this is well pleasing unto the Lord."

Ephesians 6: 1-3 "Children, obey your parents in the Lord: for this is right. Honour thy father and mother, (which is the first commandment with promise;) That it may be well with thee, and thou mayest live long on the earth."

Proverbs 22:6 "Train up a child in the way he should go: and when he is old, he will not depart from it."

Proverbs 1:8-9 "My son, hear the instruction of thy father, and forsake not the law of thy mother: For they shall be an ornament of grace unto thy head, and chains about thy neck."

Proverbs 13:24 "He that spareth his rod hateth his son: but he that loveth him chasteneth him betimes."

Proverbs 22:15 "Foolishness is bound in the heart of a child; but the rod of correction shall drive it far from him."

Proverbs 29:17 "Correct thy son, and he shall give thee rest; yea, he shall give delight unto thy soul."

Proverbs 14:26 "In the fear of the LORD is strong confidence: and his children shall have a place of refuge."

3 John 4 "I have no greater joy than to hear that my children walk in truth."

Psalm 127:3 "Lo, children are a heritage of the LORD: and the fruit of the womb is his reward."

Psalm 119:1 "Blessed are the undefiled in the way, who walk in the law of the LORD."

Proverbs 16:9 "A man's heart deviseth his way: but the LORD directeth his steps."

Deuteronomy 6:6-9 "And these words, which I command thee this day, shall be in thine heart": 7 "And thou shalt teach them diligently unto thy children and shalt talk of them when thou sittest in thine house, and when thou walkest by the way, and when thou liest down, and when thou risest up." 8 "And thou shalt bind them for a sign upon thine hand, and they shall be as frontlets between thine eyes." 9 "And thou shalt write them upon the posts of thy house, and on thy gates."

Jermiah 1:5 "Before I formed thee in the belly I knew thee; and before thou samest forth out of the womb I sanctified thee, and I ordained thee a prophet unto the nations."

James 1:17 "Every good gift and every perfect gift is from above, and cometh down from the Father of lights, with whom is no variableness, neither shadow of turning."

The scriptures I have listed represent a small fraction of what is available in the bible. Please take a look for yourself. You may use what is provided or search the scripture to find additional scriptures that will speak directly to your circumstances.

Code: Take a scripture per week and repeat it morning, noon and night with any additional times throughout the day. This process will build your faith and help you to stand on the word of God. Confess with your mouth and believe it in your heart. The results of this process will be destiny shaping. The results will shock you. The teacher will call you to say

we are not sure what has occurred, however (insert your child name) has been on good behavior and I just wanted to take a moment to phone you. See yourself receiving this call!

The Weapon of your Words (cont)

I was sitting in a meeting with Omar's teachers and school administrators to discuss his behavior. The School Administrator started the discussion highlighting the reason for this meeting was to discuss Omar's inappropriate behavior. The teachers began to discuss Omar's inability to stay on task, the constant disruptions he spearheads in the classroom, and how he will not follow directions. The entire discussion was filled with negative "Throw-in-my-face-with-no-solution" comments. I felt as if I was in a dunking tank and they continued to dunk me in the water by hitting the target with their comments. It was not that I was disagreeing or that these were allegations. I clearly understood my son was experiencing challenges. However, the discussion did not offer a ray of sunlight, hope or a moment of problem solving. After they spoke, I stated with authority, "Omar is a great student and his behavior will improve." If you allow others to speak ill about your child with no support or solutions extended, you are in agreement of this behavior continuing. This meaningless chatter has zero value and speaks no life over the situation. I also shared with the team, "I believe he needs a more conducive environment for his needs, and it starts with additional testing. It is quite overt that Omar has needs that we are not meeting. As the school administration in partnership with me as his parent, it is our responsibility to support his academic needs through assessments while equipping him the essential resources to be successful. Would you agree?" I give you, my reader friend, permission to share this same information with the administrative team during your next meeting. It clearly states we all have a job to do; let's do it!

Dr. Martin Luther King said, "If you don't stand for something you will fall for anything." I took a stand for my son. The administrators were attempting to place a label on Omar. I believe labels are designed to conceal the potential of students and adults. Although the comments were true, the delivery was not welcoming. Please do not allow anyone to speak unconstructively about your child. When sharing sensitive information such as this, it should be solution driven. Silence is acceptance, speak up and advocate for your child. When you begin to agree with the negative coupled with the deficiency of solutions, you propose agreement. When you accept labels you unconsciously accept the limitations they are placing on your child. Please understand you are not denying the existing behavior of your child. However, at the same time you are speaking life over the situation by highlighting solutions and declaring the desired behavior. Another strategic response to the teachers and administrators would be: "Thank you for bringing the concerns to my attention. While I understand (insert your child name) is currently experiencing challenges, I know he/she is a great student that possesses the capability to follow sound directions and perform well academically. Let's discuss some solutions that will support his/her needs in the classroom. My ultimate goal is to limit and eliminate his/her disruptions in the classroom with the overall focus on the academic performance. When you have encountered situations similar to this one, please share with me the plan of action steps implemented to support the student." Now, you are clearly stating you acknowledge the concerns and collaboratively we will work to uncover solutions. The stance I took in our meeting redirected a session of what's going wrong to now discuss what how we can make it right.

I believe talk is not cheap; talk can be rather expensive when it is misguided. As their guardian, you possess the power to shift the thoughts of those working directly with your child. You have the influence to shift their thinking. After this meeting, you will continue to nurture your words by showing up to the school, making calls and/or sending emails. If you are a business owner, schedule time to make a visit to your child's school as if it is an appointment with a million- dollar client. When you make your child's transformation important to you, you will notice the teachers and administrators taking a stand with you. As a result of your parental engagement, your child becomes one of their priorities. When you are engaged and involved as a parent, you receive greater support.

There is death and life in your tongue. Be sure that your words are giving life. As you share with the teachers, continue to share these thoughts with your child: "You will follow sound directions. You are a great student. You will grow up to be a productive member of society that will impact the world in a positive way. The favor of God will surround you like a shield. You will only connect with quality relationships that add good things to your life." This process will take some training within you along with the memory to do this consistently. I mentioned this again because what you do the most, you do the best. Repetition in the mother to mastery.

Do you remember a time when your child did something that was not a reflection of their upbringing? If you are anything like me, you said, "Where did this child come from?" Let's say they did not follow the teacher's instructions again. You receive a call at your office about his/her disruptive behavior. You speak with your child and your words are… "You never listen!" You will not follow directions to save your life. While this may be a reflection of what is currently happening. When speaking this over your child, you are forecasting their destiny with your words. You must confront your perception by speaking uplifting words over the circumstances. With a different perspective, your response is: "You always follow sound instructions, you are the model student in the classroom, and it is easy for you to be obedient." This weapon of words impacted my son's life so much, I began to see a new child in the same body. He transformed right before my eyes. The change did not occur overnight. However, every day I noticed a subtle change. I attribute it totally to the wisdom of God and changing my perception.

Code of Conduct: Master a positive word life. Take the test to become a word cop, do not allow anyone in your presence to speak offensively. Practice this with your child and others daily.

The Weapon of your Heart

I know what you are thinking, "Theresa is sharing with me that my heart could be used as a weapon." How? Well, I'm glad you want to know more. We have already ı with our mouth, now we must believe in our

ıe heart is the origin for every loss or gain in

, ͵   e. Whether you are using your heart weapon
consciously or unconsciously, this weapon is firing off
daily. The question… "Are you firing a loss or a gain?"
We must work together to ensure your heart is right.
Your heart must be filled with love and hope. Loving
your child when they are not so lovable and hoping for
the transformation are the keys to winning this battle.
Whatever you focus on will swell, it is vitally important
that you focus on the good only. We discussed this in the
meditation chapter. If it is not visible, make an assertive
effort to find it. If you cannot locate it, imagine it.
Imagine your child exemplifying great behavior. My
desire was to remain in the house all the time with Omar
as it was just too challenging to take him out. I would
literally talk myself through the process of taking him to
the store, mall or family gatherings. I would consistently
without fail discipline him for hitting a cousin or doing
something simply crazy while playing. After receiving a
report of Omar misbehaving, I would just sit there for a
moment with the palm of my hand holding my head
while counting to twenty. It all depended upon the crime.
This was before I began to use my weapons. I would
forecast negative behavior with my words by stating he
always misbehaves or let me take something to discipline
(belt) him with because I'm going to need it. When I
used my weapons properly, I shared with Omar before
leaving the house. I would say, "Omar, your behavior

today will be pleasing to God and your parents." We must be super cautious with our words because previously I would share with him, "Omar, be on your best behavior." Well, guess what he did? Just what I had asked of him. He was on HIS best behavior not according to my vision; it was according to his limited vision for his life. By educating him on the details of good behavior, I expanded his vision. Vision coupled with words will craft generational deposits.

Blindness builds immobility, but vision offers snapshots of the future

When we speak about the heart, I had to underscore this because words become ineffective without proper heart alignment. How do you get it in your heart? Proverbs 23:7 "For as he thinketh in his heart, so is he." It will take blending of words, actions and meditation to open your heart to new information. Did you know that your heart thinks? You need this blend of words, actions and meditation in order to obtain the preferred results. It starts with vision, what do you see. Consider the last time you desired something and initially it may appear that circumstances could potentially stand in the way. What did you do? You pushed and persevered. H. Jackson Brown Jr. said, "Sometimes the heart sees what is invisible to the eye." I believe this wholeheartedly.

Luke 6:45 reads, "A good man out of the good treasure of his heart bringeth forth that which is good; and an evil treasure of his heart bringeth forth that which is evil: for of the abundance of the heart his mouth speaketh." Your mouth tells your heart what persistently dwells on. This is why we must have full understanding that the heart is a weapon and your heart has to become the origin for gains by following these steps.

Code of conduct: Allow willingness and repetition to open your heart to receive the newness of life.

Weapon of Prayer and Fasting

With the trials of parenthood, prayer and fasting is essential to thriving through the highs and lows of life. 2 Chronicles 7:14 shares with us, "If my people, which are called by my name, shall humble themselves, and pray, and seek my face, and turn from their wicked ways; then will I hear from heaven, and will forgive their sin, and will heal their land." Prayer places the call to God and opens the lines of communication. It is calling forth your requests. "Ask, and it shall be given you; seek, and ye shall find; knock, and it shall be opened unto you." There have been countless times during a counseling session with a parent regarding the behavior of their child in which I uncovered the parent has never asked God in prayer for guidance or for the transformation of their child's behavior. If you do not set aside time to speak with God concerning your child, you will continually miss the mark. It is imperative that you couple the codes I share in this book with the instructions you receive during your prayer time. Prayer helps to build relationship while touching the heart of God. Imagine a good friend or family member that only calls when they are in need, how does that feel? Not so good. Establish a relationship with God with dedicated prayer time to avoid self-interest directed prayers.

Fasting is the planned and intentional abstinence of eating in a charge to gain spiritual equipping. Fasting helps us significantly to take control over our flesh while placing God and spirit first. One of my favorite scriptures is Matthew 6:33, "But seek ye first the kingdom of God, and his righteousness; and all these things shall be added unto you." Your capacity as a Christian is developed with a lifestyle of fasting and praying. In Matthew 17 the disciples asked Jesus why they did not possess the power to cast out demons of a man's son. Jesus responded, in Matthew 17:21, "Howbeit this kind goeth not out by prayer and fasting." Prayer and Fasting gives us another level of power.

Code of Conduct: Set aside time daily for prayer and seek God regarding your fasting lifestyle. God may share with you to fast twice a week, twice a month or more. Create a lifestyle of prayer and fasting and expect greater revelation and power.

Carry and fire your weapons daily in the most positive imaginable way. Allow your imagination to impact your faith. Hebrews 11:1, "Now faith is the substance of things hoped for, the evidence of things not seen."

Journal (Be sure to include prayer revelations)

CHAPTER 8

INCLEMENT WEATHER

Inclement Weather is inevitable just as trials. 1 Peter 4:12 denotes, "Beloved, think it not strange concerning the fiery trial which is to try you, as though some strange thing happened unto you. In this lifetime, we will not live trial-free." What is really important is our perspective towards the trial. My mentor, Dr. Traci Lynn, speaks around the nation about the significance of your attitude and thinking. She said, "Changing your thinking will change your living."

It is raining cats and dogs (as if you have ever seen cats and dogs raining). Anyway, there are heavy rains. What is your outlook of the day? Is it suddenly gloomy because of the inclement weather? Do you view the rain as an interruption or as liquid sunshine? Perspective is packed with power; our thought life will make or break our day, month, year and even life. The goal is to shift every negative into a positive. I have trained myself on positive thinking, so much that I unconsciously translate every unpleasant occurrence into a pleasant one. Also recognize every code outlined involves training of yourself and your child.

Whatever you fail to train, you have no right to complain
– Dr. Mike Freeman

As you begin to implement the steps I am sharing with you. There will be trials, however your outlook of the trial will be the determining factor. Omar spent the weekend with my sister Nikki and niece Temica when he was an 8-year-old. I was at work when I received the urgent call from Nikki. She was frantic as she told me they called an ambulance, and would be transporting Omar to the emergency room because he would not stop having seizures. I rushed from work to the hospital praying all the way there. When I arrived to the emergency room, Omar's eyes were glazed and he was non-responsive. I continued to speak to him anyway because my perspective was he can hear me and he will be just fine. I told him in a calming tone, "Omar you will be fine. Remember, God is with you and he will help you through this." Again he began to shake uncontrollably and his eyes rolled back. His lips began to turn blue and the monitors began to beep loudly. The doctor and additional nurses rushed into the room. The doctor said, "Mom we are going to have to ask you to step out for a moment and the nurse will come to get you shortly." "Oh my word, you want who to do what? I'm his mother I should be able to stay," I replied. Tears began to run down my face again as Nikki softly grabbed my hand to escort me to the waiting room. I was trying really hard to keep it together. We walked out, and the entire time I was looking to see what they were doing with my son.

We entered the waiting room and I could not sit down. As I was pacing the floor, a voice spoke over the intercom announcing a code blue. I said, NO! NO! NO! This was extremely challenging for me, and was truly beckoning my faith. Nikki, Temica, and I held hands as Nikki began to pray. The presence of Holy Spirit helped me to grab and hold on to the proper perspective. It is equally important to surround yourself with the right people. Your circle will persuade your perspective. I started to pray and I am quite certain the visitors and patients on the 12th floor could hear me clearly. My perspective was not going to be altered by what I saw or the announcement made. I knew with my heart-sight, my baby was going to be fine. Proverbs 3:5-6, "Trust in the LORD with all thine heart; and lean not unto thine own understanding. In all thy ways acknowledge him, and he shall direct thy paths." This is exactly the stance I took that day. As I mentioned when the trials come, maintain the proper perspective and watch the manifestation.

Omar remained in the hospital for a few days. My mom, dad and family visited daily. My spiritual parents Bishop and First Lady Mitchum visited Omar as well and prayed with us. After prayer and proper perspective, Omar was released in good health and returned to school as if the hospital scare never occurred.

Code of Conduct: Your perspective is the umbrella and suit you need in the heaviest storms of life. It plays the lead role in the outcome of the trials you face. Do yourself a service by starting with the miniature trials to cultivate that optimistic perspective. When the major trials come, you know and understand the influence of the proper response. Practice makes progress and perfection.

Journal

CHAPTER 9

COMMUNITY SERVICE

Blessed are the givers! The more you sow into the lives of others, the greater the harvest you will reap. I continue to donate countless hours to my church and community initiatives. Whatever you stand in need of, you should give more of. If you have ever compared your child to another child, this is a great opportunity to appreciate and be grateful for your blessings. Volunteer at a shelter, at a church, rehabilitation center or just to an individual or family in need. There is always someone or a family with twice the responsibility as you and hear this. . .they have mastered the right perspective with a spirit of Thanksgiving.

When you are appreciative for what you have, it centers you in a posture of gratitude. It will shift the focus from what is missing in your life. At the beginning of my parenting journey, I would notice high performing well behaved students in the classroom. I would say to myself, this is how I intended Omar to show up in life. As a consequence, this made me extremely sad and focused on inadequacy. I began to transform my thoughts and reposition my focus. When I started to extract and spotlight the things we are thankful for, it made me strong. I understand my son is special and unique just as your child. There will never ever be another child like yours and that is what separates us from others. Joshua 1:9, "Have not I commanded thee? Be strong and of good courage; be not afraid, neither be thou dismayed: for the LORD thy God is with thee whithersoever thou goest."

Code of Conduct: Another aspect of serving God is serving others. Our service to others pleases God. Serving others not only blessings others, it blesses us more. Make a conscious effort to live a life of serving.

Journal

CHAPTER 10

GRADUATION

Congratulations! It is graduation time.

This new chapter of your life will be written by you. I have shared the codes I implemented which transitioned my son from the problem child to the model student. I wish I had the Parent Code of Conduct book in my life, it would have accelerated our winning outcome. I believe and stand in agreement with you for the victory your family has already received in the spirit. We now thank God for the earthly manifestation. This is your opportunity to denote all that you are currently witnessing with your eyesight, the improvements made during you reading and what you expect to occur very soon in the life of your child. It is my prayer that the codes shared in this book will serve as the catalyst to transforming your child's behavior.

My new chapter:

_____

_____

_____

_____

_____

_____

_____

_____

_____

_____

_____

_____

_____

_____

_____

_____

_____

_____

_____

_____

_____

_____

_____

_____

_____

_____

_____

_____

If you desire to receive more and participate in workshops and tele-seminars, please sign up to stay connected on www.parentcodeofconduct.com to receive updates. Check out additional helpful products on the website.

My team and I also desire to hear from you. Please share your phenomenal testimonies in writing or video by email: info@parentcodeofconduct.com.

ABOUT THE AUTHOR

Theresa Roulhac Proctor, a minister, Diamond and Presidential Founder with Traci Lynn Jewelry, motivational speaker, author, philanthropist, national trainer, wife and mother.

Theresa has mastered the law of value by compelling others to move into their purpose while operating in their gifts. Through her leadership, thousands continue to benefit from greater self confidence, debt elimination, a flowing wealth stream and ultimately a life transformed.

Shining in talents of negotiation, diplomacy and collaborative work, she has serves as an influential Board Member with a number of non profit organizations that support issues she treasures.

Theresa finds fulfillment in serving God and spending time with family. Parenting is an assignment in which she takes to heart. As a parent of a child with special needs, she passionately shares her struggles and strategies implemented to transition a problem child to a model student.

There are those who leave it to others and there are those who take it upon themselves to make a difference. Theresa Roulhac Proctor is undoubtedly a difference maker filled with impact, action and phenomenal results.

The best parents equip themselves with more information. Subscribe to more resources: www.parentcodeofconduct.com

Made in the USA
Charleston, SC
01 June 2014